AF271414

THE GIRL WITH
THE BROKEN SPIRIT

By

Martin D Gangley

Copyright © 2022 by Martin D Gangley

All rights reserved. This book or any portion thereof may not be reproduced or used in any manner whatsoever without the express written permission of the publisher except for the use of brief quotations in a book review.

Printed in the United States of America

First Printing, 2022

EBOOK ISBN: 978-969-2592-79-6

PAPERBACK ISBN: 978-969-2592-80-2

TABLE OF CONTENTS

TABLE OF CONTENTS

CHAPTER 1

Intake

Emaria woke up that day disoriented, and late.

Why? She could not remember. She only had these vague, but persisting, images at the back of her mind that she could not place. She had an inkling that something important, or even life changing, might have had happened last night, she just couldn't put a finger on the specifics.

'Oh well… if it was something important enough, it will come back to me once again.' she supposed, chalking her hazy memory up to the insane amount of drinking she had partaken in last night.

Nothing new there either, it was normal. Routine even.

She had these nights filled with elusive moments at least once a week now, if not more than that. And no matter how hard she tried, the memories stayed out of her reach.

'Maybe I should really cut back on the drinking...' she thought, knowing damn well that she would not be making good on those thoughts, as always. Come morning, she would be waking up just as hungover.

So she put the nagging feeling of something amiss at the back of her mind and proceeded to get ready for the day ahead of her. She had an important meeting later in the day, something she had been working on for a long time now, and if everything went according to plan, she might even be getting a promotion out of it. So keeping her fingers crossed, she dressed to impress and set out to work.

She took the bus to the work, as she always did, and she hated every second of it, again, as she always did. It brought very unwanted memories and very uncomfortable feelings at the forefront of her head. Something she had learned to live with, but still not accepted, because unfortunately, that was the only time efficient way for her to move about.

'*Maybe I really should think of renting a bike for work...*' she thought. But she knew this thought will also never come to fruition, as the ones preceding it had never had. And she didn't always hate traveling through the public transport, it was just on the bad days. And unfortunately that day was also one of them.

She forced herself to calm down and look out the window, just enjoying the sights as they passed by. New Orleans was a pretty place to see anyway. Magical even, if only you had the eyes to see the magic scattered all over the place. The streets, the shops, the cozy nooks and crannies, everything was magical.

Soon enough her admiring spiel of her surrounding was cut short as she reached her work place. She squared her shoulders, took a large, calming breath and entered the building.

It was time to put her professional face on.

She met the boss, the colleagues and the friends she had at work, all with the same energy as she always did. She gave the presentation that she was supposed and it was banging. And she still, at the end of it all, got the impression that she might not be the one getting that promotion after all.

'Maybe it's not a good thing that all your colleagues know you as a raging alcoholic.' She thought resignedly. 'Not when most of your drinking buddies are your work buddies too.'

'Well it's not like I am going to just stop now so... whatever'

She let out a sigh and left the meeting room, a little despondently.

'Maybe I can convince Dwayne and Savannah to go out tonight?' To celebrate the successful presentation at least, if not promotion.' She thought a little contemplatively and immediately cheered up. It was a good reason to go out and have some fun.

And Dwayne and Savannah were always up for some fun. They were good friends of her so going out with them was sure to guarantee a great time for all them.

With that thought in mind, she hurried to talk to them and as always, they were game. Later that day, after they were done with the work day, they all headed to a local pub to have their dinner.

Their next destination of the night was the Bourbon Street.

And it was a damn good destination. They spent most of their time there, drinking and dancing and it was around midnight when Amaria came back home.

Exhausted and drunk.

She immediately changed and had a glass of water, the experience had taught her that that would really help her when she would wake up miserable in the morning. She absolutely did not want to wake up dehydrated as well as hungover again. That sucked.

After chugging down a glass of water, she headed straight to her bed and proceeded to almost drop on it.

And then, out came the monsters she kept hiding behind her happy demeanor the whole day. As she lay on the bed, there was no one left to see the smile dropping off from her face and replaced by the emptiness in her eyes. She was alone in her house, with nothing to keep her company except some random noise of the night that sometimes filtered in from the street outside.

She laid there for a long, long time; just thinking about her life, or lack thereof. She did not think she had any life left in her.

Sometimes she felt like nothing but an empty shell that only held the bad memories and the traumas of the past in it.

Sometimes she did not even have enough to think about. And then she would spend an hour thinking about that. What was there to live for anyway? She would think and then would not find any answer to that question. She would keep thinking about that, looking for an answer long and wide until her eyelids would start to droop with tiredness and sleep.

It was one of those nights.

Exhausted, she closed her eyes and gave in to the sleep.

The next time she woke up, she was sure the things had taken an unexpected turn.

For better or for worse? It was yet to be seen.

CHAPTER 2

Falling Into a Nightmare

Emaria woke up that day disoriented, again.

Only this time around she had a really good reason for the said disorientation.

She hadn't woken up that day where she had gone to sleep last night. She also did not wake up as she had gone to sleep.

She had gone to sleep in her room, at her own apartment, alone and drunk and wallowing in her self-pity, and she had woken up in a bed that decidedly wasn't the she had dropped in last night. It did not feel huge enough, and it certainly wasn't soft enough to be hers. Moreover, she was woken up because of the harsh glare of sun, filtering through a huge ass window. Something she definitely did not have in her room.

She looked down at her body, only to see a t-shirt and shorts adorning it. That too was very out of place. She did not remember ever changing out of her work clothes last night.

She sat up groggily and got out of the bed. And she immediately stumbled on her feet, as if her center of gravity was immensely misplaced. Catching a hold of herself, she straightened up to get to the door so as to get some answers about her whereabouts. It was very puzzling to say the least.

'Did I sleep walk somewhere? Did I got to someone else's place last night and didn't remember it? Did someone change my clothes!?' She tried to make some sense of it all but couldn't, there was no right scenario that came up. No matter how drunk she was, this had never happened before.

'Is it another side effect of drinking or something? Am I having blackouts now?' She wondered.

Her musings were cut short, however, when she came face to face with a mirror on the wall she was passing by to get to the door. She immediately halted in her steps and just stared in the mirror for a good solid minute. Slack jawed with shock.

And then, immediately screamed.

Because... forget the different room and the different clothes, she was in a different body altogether. She did not even look like herself when she had last seen the mirror. And no, the person staring back at her wasn't any stranger either. It was a face she was immensely familiar with. It was a face she saw every day, just not quite how she was seeing it at the moment. It was a face she knew as well as her own because... it was her own face. Still, not quite. It was the face she saw every day when she looked in the mirror, and not exactly at the same time.

It was a face of her of the time long past.

Because, Amaria had gone to sleep as a 25 year old adult woman, having just celebrated her birthday a week ago, but now... now she was looking at the face of her 14 years old self. In her 14 years old body.

And now come to think of it... the room she had woken up in, it was her old bedroom. A place she hadn't been in for more than half a decade now.

So yeah... the screaming that she was doing? Perfectly reasonable.

Very understandable even.

But apparently, not to everyone.

Her screaming was rudely interrupted by a loud bang. It was the sound of the door being swung open. That loud bang was immediately followed by a woman's cross tirade.

"What the hell are you screaming about this early in the morning, girl!?"

Ah, her dear old mother.

She kept on berating Amaria while she was just busy staring at her, not really listening to the words coming out of her mouth, instead just taking her in. The last time she had seen her mother was over a year ago, and that too was at someone's wedding. They hadn't talked to each other much then, preferring to ignore each other.

And now, standing in front of the formidable woman, in the body of her 14 year old self, made her feel 14 again. Small, helpless and really scared.

It brought unprompted tears to her eyes.

"Mom..." she whispered, a little unsure, a little broken.

The mom in question, however, did not even seem to hear her. She was still saying something to her so Amaria tuned in once again.

"… and stop wasting time! Why are you still standing here like a statue!? Go get ready for the school." She ended her long spiel, giving Amaria a lost once over and immediately turning around, and went out of the room. Slamming the door behind her with a resounding echo.

Leaving Amira alone in her room.

Hastily wiping tears from her cheeks, embarrassed that she had even started crying in the first place.

And that's when she realized, she was feeling everything as if it was real. The emotions, the surroundings and even her own touch, all of it felt real. Too real to be dream as she had initially thought it to be.

Because yes, she had. That's what her mind had supplied at every turn on event. When she saw herself in the mirror or even when she had seen her mother, she had been trying to convince herself at the back of her mind that it was all a dream.

That everything she was seeing wasn't actually happening in reality.

That her mind, subconscious one at that, had just conjured everything up.

That did not seem to be the case actually.

Everything felt too real to be true.

Too detailed to be just a figment of her imagination.

And that's when she started hyperventilating.

This was too big to just keep it to herself and just go with the flow. She needed to tell someone. She needed to get some help. As soon as she had thought that, she thought of her mother.

'Yes...' she thought. 'I have to tell mom. I have to get help.'

"Mom..." she shouted for the second time that day and rushed out of her doorway, in search of some help.

CHAPTER 3

A Light in the Darkness

Talking to her mother hadn't gone as well as she had hoped, and that was as massive an understatement as there ever was. It had gone downright horrible.

First off, her mother was still cross with her at being rudely interrupted during her usual morning routine, which usually consisted of her having her breakfast, which in turn, consisted mostly of something or the other alcoholic. And reading the paper.

And then her mother was not very appreciative of her 'blown way out of proportion dramatics', or so she said. In reality, it was just desperate attempts of Amaria to get her mother to understand that she was a full grown ass adult up until last night and now she was trapped in her teenage body. Her mother did not understand that at all. Which was understandable, really. It wasn't everyday something of this magnitude happened. And it was certainly not everyone that could attest to having the same experience, but, her mother didn't have to go as far as accusing her of lying. Just to get out of going to school?

'Couldn't she have at least listened to me and just tried to understand what I was trying to say?' Amaria thought despondently.

But even as she was thinking that she came to realize that it really was a long shot, for her to think that her mother would ever be on her side. In anything. She had almost forgotten how that felt like over the years that she had been away from her mother.

Her mother, Lucia, had always cut an imposing figure in her life. She had never been loving or caring, let alone nourishing in any way whatsoever. She was mostly distant. Cold and uncaring, as if she was far removed from her life. Sometimes, when she was in a mood of hers, for one reason or another, she would even unload that on Amaria. Not physically, never physically, but some words had the power to hurt deeper than anything physical ever could. And Amaria had been thrown such words a lot in her life, almost always from her mother.

With time, Amaria had learned how to live with the wounds her mother had inflicted on her. Never healed, just hidden. Hell she hadn't even fully forgotten, there was a reason she seldom met or talked to her mother, but still being in the face of that wrath was bringing up many unpleasant memories.

And God, had she forgotten the stench of alcohol that always followed around her mother. Now coming face to face with the walking reminder was enough for Amaria to wonder if that same smell followed her around too now.

Shaking her head at the dark turn her thoughts had taken, Amaria came to a stop outside the school building.

Her old school building.

Yes she was here to actually go to school and attend classes and all that.

Why? Because her mother had forced her too.

No matter how much she protested or argued with her mother, she hadn't been heard. Her mother had simply asked her to cut her act and get ready for school.

15

And now Amaria was standing in front of that said school.

She gave the building a once over. It was a place that had been the source of her happiness as well as her immense anguish once upon a time. Just looking at it brought along many memories, some good that she wouldn't mind revisiting and some so bad she'd rather die than going through once again.

But well, she was here now, and she still hadn't the faintest idea about what to do next. She still did not know what the hell was happening and just going with the flow of the things seemed to be the best course of action at the moment. So she decided to do just that.

She took a deep breath and stepped into the school.

It was just as she had remembered and not quite as she remembered at the same time. The school grounds weren't as huge as she had thought them to be. The school hallways weren't as crowded as her mind supplied, they were much more crowded in reality. The classroom ceiling wasn't as high as she recalled. Some alcoves weren't as tiny or hidden as she once thought they were.

All in all, it was a bizarre occurrence. Almost like an out of body experience.

'Maybe that's what it is. An out of body experience. Maybe I'm just going through my memories or something? They are just really hyper realistic.' she wondered thoughtfully.

Her musings were cut short when she heard a loud yell of her name.

"Amaria! Hey! Here, Ams…" It was a male voice. And it was very familiar.

She whirled around to catch look at the face behind the voice.

"Kevin…" she whispered out loud. It was Kevin, her best friend, waving at her, trying to catch her attention.

Before she could get over her surprise at seeing the 14 year old version of him once again in flesh, right front of her eyes, she spotted another figure right beside him.

"Gabriella…" she muttered again, doubly shocked.

Although it didn't make sense for her to be surprised, of course they were going to be here. They went to the same school! Why hadn't she thought about that before?

Honestly, it was because they had gotten a bit out of touch over the years, especially after both of them had moved to different states, Gabriella after her marriage and Kevin for his job. They did meet up or talked sometimes but that was in passing and far in between.

But once they had been the best thing that happened to her. They had been together through thick and thin, all since preschool. They were there for each other whenever one of them needed help. When Kevin had lost his father or when Gab had gotten in an accident or when her boyfriend was being a dick. Or when Amaria had...

Amariar visibly shuddered at the thoughts her mind had taken to and focused on the reality. Or as much of a reality as this whole situation was.

On her friends, yes. On some of the darker days, their friendship was the only thing that had given her the will and the strength to go on.

And seeing them there together with huge smiles and hands waving at her, urging her to come join them, Amaria found the comfort she had been looking for.

And she promptly burst into tears.

Their shocked and worried faces pushed her even more on the edge and by the time they had reached her, she was in hysterics. She promptly flung herself at them and babbled on and on about growing up and growing apart and waking up in a dream.

As expected, they did not understand her one bit. But they were certainly more concerned than her mother.

That concern of them was what made them bring her to the principal's office. Patting her, consoling her and comforting her all the way there. She could have cried anew just at that if she wasn't already bawling her heart out.

It was a bittersweet moment for her.

The meeting with the principal was not very bittersweet, however. It was anything but.

The flood gates of her eyes had stopped but her word vomit did not. Once she started talking about her predicament, she did not hold back. It took her an hour to go through that conversation. Soon her friends were sent to class while she was left in the principal's office alone with him.

'At least I don't have to take a class now...' she thought with a wry twist to her lips.

The principal had just sat there letting her let out all her emotions. He hadn't stopped her from talking. Hadn't interrupted her while she was retelling the whole last night's happenings.

He hadn't even called her dramatic or a liar.

He had quietly said, after she was done talking and sobbing and was just minutely hiccupping every once in a while;

"Oh you must be feeling very overwhelmed my dear. And I know just the person who can help you. In fact, let me call that gentleman right here."

With that he turned to his phone and quietly asked for some one. A name Amaria could not make out clearly.

But with the tone the principal had taken, she wasn't sure what to expect. So she just sat there, waiting and hoping for a damn miracle.

It was about 5 minutes later when the door to the principal's office opened once again. The person that entered the room was the last person Amaria would have ever guessed.

But still, she had inkling that this might really be the answer to all her questions. Or just the opposite of that.

"Dr. Martin…" she whispered, anticipation and trepidation, both clear in her voice.

Called The Girl With The Broken Spirit

CHAPTER 4

Assessment

"Dr. Martin...!" exclaimed Amaria, springing out of her seat at once at seeing another familiar face.

"Yes. That's me. But I don't seem to recall a name to put with your face, Miss...?" he replied, looking mildly confused but still mostly curious.

Ah yes, she had forgotten that tiny bit of detail in her excitement at seeing a familiar face. He had never been a familiar face for her when she was younger. She had gotten to know him later on in life, just around 3 years or so ago in fact. So his surprise at her easy familiarity was perfectly understandable.

"Garcia. This is Miss Garcia, Dr. Martin. And Miss Garcia, this is Doctor Martin. Our resident... psychology counselor, you could say. Doctor, I think Miss Garcia here might be in need of your assistance." Amaria was just thinking about how to better

23

answer the doctor's question when the Principal himself beat her to it. She whirled around instantly at the sound of his voice, almost having forgotten just where she was at the moment and what was she doing.

Her mind was quick to catch his words even through the haze of the momentary shock.

"What? What do you mean his help? Do you think I am crazy or something? I'm not! I am not crazy! And I do not need a bloody shrink right now!" she immediately exploded at the man upon realizing what he was insinuating, ready to throw hands if need be.

To his credit the principal remained perfectly calm through all that and only continued to tread gently as if dealing with a spooked animal.

"I understand my dear. Believe me I do. I know you really believe what you take to be the truth and I get that but, I really think this is in the best interest of you and your future, child." He tried to be placating, and calm her down but Amaria was having none of it. If anything, it made her even more furious, being treated as a stupid kid.

"I am not a bloody child, for God's sake! Stop calling me that! And stop treating me like one too!" Amaria shouted, banging her hands on the table in front of her and causing some figurines to fly off the table. There was a resounding crash and the sound of shattering glass that accompanied it. She had definitely broken something, possibly valuable but she was beyond care.

She was frustrated so beyond belief now that tears had once again sprung up in her eyes.

"Uh... if I may... Miss Garcia was it?" started Dr. Martin tentatively. Amaria whirled around to focus on him this time. Nodding her head to show that he could go on.

"I think you should really have a discussion with a professional, if only to just make sure that you really are alright. Don't you want to prove that you are not... crazy... as you put it? I can help you prove it to everyone." He ended, adding just a little bit of hope and encouragement in his words.

And dang it!

She knew that the man was being downright manipulative. She had known him for like 3 years already so she also knew all his little gives. The little tricks he uses to pull in the people and make them trust him. But she also knew that it was really only for the purpose of helping others. And clearly he was trying to do the same with her too.

He was only trying to help her.

With that knowledge in mind, all the fight seemingly left Amaria and she let out a defeated sigh. Already waiting for the day to end. And the nightmare to stop.

But alas that was not to be. She still had most of the day to live through no matter how done she was with it. And who knew for how long she would be trapped in the nightmare anyway?

"Amaria" she started with a low tone, tired. "My name is Amaria Dr. Martin. You should really know my first name at least, if we're actually going to do this."

"Of course Miss Amaria." He replied, just as comforting.

"So lead the way doctor. To your office." She said finally getting to the door. Just as she was to cross the threshold she turned back to the principal once again.

"Thank you for your help, Sir." She said a little sarcastically, but also a little gratefully.

"Of course my dear. It's what I'm here for anyway." He replied jovially, a smile playing on his lips, as if all the crying and the shouting of the last hour hadn't even happened.

With that Amaria set to follow the psychiatrist to his office in silence, using the time it took to reach there to better categorize her thoughts and emotions. She really did not want to come off as actually insane, and for that she needed to keep her wits about the situation and not delve into hysterics again.

She came across some faces in the hallways, some she recognized and some she did not, and almost all of them gave her weird and curious looks. She couldn't fault them for that. She couldn't imagine the sight that she was presenting at the moment, definitely red and blotchy and there were sure to be tear tracks and snot on her face somewhere after more than an hour of crying and screaming. And she was sure some of them had actually seen her dramatic breakdown earlier. And combine it with the fact that she was walking with the school psychiatrist.

Yeah, none of it painted a pretty picture for the impressionable teens. But she could not, for the life of her, bring herself to actually care about those stares.

She had a much bigger problem at hand.

And she was sure she was going to spend another hour and two in the company of that said doctor. Just hopefully there wouldn't be any shouting or crying anymore. It was already a long enough day.

With that they had reached the doctor's office. And yes, Amaria was right. It was a long, long day for her.

The next time she came out of that office it was after two hours. With even more tear tracks and snot. With even more red rimmed and angry eyes.

She had told him everything that had happened to her. Everything of her past that she thought might be of importance. She had told him about how she was a 25 year old adult and how she had just gone to sleep in her own bed after getting pissed last night. She had told him how she had woken up as a 14 year old. And how she remembered everything from her older life.

It had not gone how she had thought it would. And the most important reason for that was the fact this Dr. Martin was not the Dr. Martin that she was used to. This man did not know her.

This man hadn't been with her through with many of her bouts of depression. He did not know who she was.

And no matter how much she tried to convince him, he remained unconvinced. He had really tried to not show that he wasn't buying anything that she was saying. But as she had realized earlier, she knew all his tells. So she knew when he was agreeing with her and when he was just pretending to agree. So as to not spook her. So as to keep her calm.

As if she was demented patient. A time bomb that could go off at any moment if he did not tread carefully around her.

He had said she might have just dreamt it all up and that some people had really active imagination, after her insistence to at least tell her what he thought might be wrong with her. According to him, some people tend to conjure up whole worlds and lives, especially if their own is not very satisfactory. She had laughed out loud at his face at that and then had cursed him some.

He had just smiled amiably in return as if both of them were in on the joke.

She was not.

She wanted to rip her hair out in frustration, or maybe his. Yeah definitely his. But she refrained. Violence was never the answer.

She had just screamed some more, despite her earlier promise to herself to not do that. She had also ended up breaking some of his things too in a fit of rage and despair. That did help some but it would have helped her vindictive soul even more if the bastard hadn't just sat calmly through it all.

She had then tried telling him the things that she knew about him, his name, his birthday, his parents' names, his address, his girlfriend's name and what not. That hadn't helped her argument either.

Some of them were just not true for him yet, like his address. And some of them were just public knowledge although Amaria could tell that he was a little creeped out at the fact that she knew all that. She was after all just a teenage girl that he had never met before.

In the end, it had gone nowhere. Her assessment, as it was called.

None of us was willing to concede to the other. So he just told her to just try and relax and not stress anymore about it. He had told her to just spend the day like usual and that they should schedule other sessions in the future to better understand her thoughts.

She had said good riddance and left his office at once.

Unfortunately, she had no idea how she used to spend the day usually when she was 14.

Fortunately, she had gotten permission to skip the school and go home for the day to rest. She took up that offer and almost bolted from the school.

Only she didn't want to go home either so she spent the day roaming the area, taking in the places she used to visit in her child. Places she sometimes missed in her adult life.

It was a bittersweet day for her.

When she finally went home in the evening, her mother was already there but she just left her alone, for once. Most probably the school had contacted her and told her about her daughter's breakdown. And instead of comforting her she just gave her a wide berth and kept to herself. Not something many mothers would do, but at least she wasn't all up in her face and shouting at her. So that was something.

Later that night, she had dinner and quietly went to sleep. All the while thinking about what to do next and how to tackle this sudden chance of reliving her teenage.

When she woke up the next morning, there sunlight coming through. There were no windows to let the light in.

Instead, she woke up to her blaring alarm. Reminding her that she needed to get up for work.

CHAPTER 5

THE MORNING AFTER

Amaria woke up that day with the ringing of the alarm clock, and a pounding headache to accompany it.

It took her a minute or so to catch her bearings, but everything started coming back to her immediately when she realized where she was. Or more appropriately, where she was not, anymore. She was in her own apartment, in her own room. Not the one she had when she was 14, but the one she had in her adult life. When she was 25.

She threw off her covers in a hurry, only to see that yes, she was in her grown up body, wearing her grown up dress. Still, she just had to make sure so she rushed to the bathroom to look at herself in the mirror. And yes, now it was confirmed. She was not a 14 year old girl, she was a 25 year old woman.

But what the hell had been... whatever that it had been?

Was it a dream?

Seriously? Did she just dream a whole ass another life? And that too as her younger self? A time in her life that she hated. And did her mother just had to be there too? A person she had tried to remove herself from the hardest. What were the odds of that happening? None at all. Or so she had thought. But apparently that was not the case…? Because it had just occurred.

She couldn't wrap her head around what had happened to her.

She rushed to check the date and the time, to confirm that she hadn't just spent an entire day someplace else, and no, she hadn't. It was the very next day, right after the night she had gone to sleep. So no, she could not possibly be living another life.

That was not possible.

She shook her head, trying to get rid of the ridiculous dream and all the stupid thoughts that it had brought along with it. Because that's what it was. And she could just forget it and move pat it like she had been doing with her previous dreams.

With that sudden thought, she came to an abrupt halt.

Because, now that she was thinking about it, she had started realizing some things that she had missed earlier. Or chose to miss them, not thinking of them of any importance.

Because, it wasn't the first time it had happened to her, was it?

No, it was not.

It had been going on for a while. In fact, now that she thought about it really hard, it had started over a week ago. It had started the day she had turned 25. Or more like on the night of her 25th birthday. She was so high off partying and having fun with her friends, celebrating her birthday, that she had paid it no mind.

And then it had started happening every night after that.

Most of the time when she went to sleep she would be tired beyond belief, or really just drunk beyond her wits, so she never stopped to think clearly and deeply about it. And even when she did, she chalked it up to vague dreams.

But now, all the muddied, unclear dreams that she had been having as of late, they were starting to come back to her now. In all their clarity.

And in all of them, she had woken up in a different world.

And in all of them she was 14.

And in all of them she was having either an out of body experience, a panic attack or a row with her mother.

Yeah, that explained why her mother was shouting at her so much. Because it hadn't been the first time it had happened. It was most probably the 3rd time, her meeting with her mother. In other versions of the dream she would either just wake up to look around, confused at her surroundings, or just try to make any sense of her whereabouts.

But during none of those times had it transpired further than that. It was her first time, spending a whole day as her teenage self.

But the fact of the matter remained. It was not normal. Something definitely was going on with her.

Was she losing her mind?

Unnerved and very out of depth, she did the only thing that came to her mind. She called Dr. Martin. Her doctor Martin, of the present time. He picked up the phone after a while and from the surprise and concern in his tone, she realized that it was far too early for someone to be hitting up their psychiatrist. But, what else could she do? She couldn't think of anything else.

Sensing her confusion and panic, Dr. Martin tried to calm her down and told her that she could come to see him in his office whenever she could, he would meet her there.

Letting out a sigh of relief at his kindness, she hung up and got up to get ready to go see him.

But before that, she quickly called up her office. She had to call in sick for the day. She did not think she would be able to go through a normal work day after the day she had just gone through. Or the night she had just gone through…?

Ah that was getting really confusing. And she needed to find answers.

As soon as she possibly could.

Called The Girl With The Broken Spirit

CHAPTER 6

ASSESSMENT 2

Amaria wasted no time in getting to the doctor's office. In fact, she was pretty sure that she was the first person through his office doors, after him of course. And boy was she relieved, seeing him in front of her, in the flesh.

She hadn't seen him for over a month now but still, it felt like she had just seen him yesterday. And the type of day, or night rather, that she had just had, that feeling did not sit well with her. It made her even more anxious and jittery.

By the time she had entered his office, she was having a full on panic attack, hyperventilating and trembling like a leaf. Dr. Martin was sitting on his chair when she had entered but on seeing her condition, he got up in the blink of an eye, rushing to her and guiding her towards the couch. He made her sit down and then focused on getting her breathing under control and calming her down. He let her have her moment and come back to her senses in her own time while he just sat there close to her, letting her know that she was not alone.

As soon as her breathing became regular once again, he got her a glass of water.

She almost gulped the whole glass of water down in one go, spilling some on herself and on the couch because of her shaking hands. But she did not care that she was creating a mess.

She was beyond care at that point.

As soon as she was in a little more control of her body once again, she almost pounced on the doctor, who was crouching on the floor in front of her, grabbing him by his arm she stood up, bringing him up along with her.

"Dr. Martin! You have to help me! I had this weird dream… and I keep having these dreams… and I was 14… and then there was my mother there when I woke up and she was shouting at me… she was just so awful… and I went to the school and it was all so horrible too! And you were there too! But you did not know me… and… and I broke your vase. I'm sorry, I didn't mean to but you didn't even believe me... and then I..." once she had started talking, there was no stopping her.

She kept on rambling, getting everything off her chest and Dr. Martin let her ramble on until she had said everything that came to her mind.

Dr. Martin knew that she needed to say all that, and go on until she was drained of all the nervous energy trapped in her body. It would really be helpful for her, lying getting rid of a huge weight on your chest, even if he did not understand everything that she was saying. So far he had only heard the words like a dream, a school, the shouting mother, and of course the part where she said she had broken his vase.

He did not remember her doing that but he still turned to his side to look back at his desk, surreptitiously of course, just to make sure that his vase was still there. It was his favorite one after all!

But that was going off topic, he turned to the now crying girl and made her sit down once again, sitting beside her on the couch. After she was all cried out, he gave her the tissues that were kept handy, right beside the couch.

"OK, Now that that's all over, can you start from the beginning once again love. I'm afraid I did not quite catch everything that you just said. And take your time. There's no hurry. We have got all day." He said to her gently, making sure to come across as just curious and not condescending. She hated that.

She took a deep breath and started once again, slowly and from the beginning this time.

She told him how she had started having these weird dreams a week ago but she always forgot them when she woke up. She told him how last night, during her dream, she had lived through a whole day as another person. And not just any person, her very own younger self.

She told him about him too, he doctor Martin of her dream world, and that did seem an awful lot like him. But then again, she had known him a long time, she could probably guess his reactions to any situation by now, so he couldn't just base an opinion on that fact.

She also told him about how sleeping in one reality had made her wake up in the other one and she had woken up in the real world only after she had gone to sleep as her dream self.

The plot kept thickening.

While she was telling him everything, Dr. Martin was focused on the emotions passing through her face as well as focusing on her words. It was a hard task but he was well practiced. He couldn't always just believe on every word his patients said to him. He had to look for their little tells that showed him whether they were lying or actually being truthful.

And what he had known of Amaria and what he was seeing her going through right now, he knew without a shadow of a doubt, that she was telling the absolute truth.

Or what she believed to be the absolute truth, at least.

Oh boy, did he have a long day ahead of him!

Called The Girl With The Broken Spirit

CHAPTER 7

INTERLUDE

Amaria got home pretty late in the day after her meeting with Dr. Martin. And, with far more new questions than the answers.

Her sitting with the doc hadn't gone as well as she had hoped for it to go. Now, don't get her wrong, Dr. Martin was just as kind and supportive as he had always been, it was just that... he seemed to be coming to the same conclusions that his counterpart had been.

That something was wrong with her.

She got that. She already knew that. But, it didn't seem to be as simple as that.

Because the consensus was that something was wrong with her, mentally.

Like she was going crazy.

Doctor Martin hadn't said that outright but she had gathered that much from his tone and his remarks. Remarks of monitoring her sleep routine and trying a sleep medication, as well as cutting back on alcohol consumption. She knew she was a certified alcoholic, just like her mom had been so she had her to thank for her addiction, but it didn't mean that she could just start shifting bodies and timelines because of that. She had never heard of alcohol causing all that, no matter how much drunk you got.

Doctor Martin was under the impression that she might be suffering from a personality disorder or a dissociative identity disorder. But that's where he was wrong. You see, personality disorders and identity disorders can surely make you feel like a new person, but they can't just make you look like another person too. And she wasn't *feeling* 14, she was actually in the body of her 14 year old self. Feeling wise, she had still been 25, just trapped in another body.

She had seen the mirror, there was no mistaking that.

And there was no time lost in her memories, there was no discrepancies in timing. It wasn't like she had spent the whole day as 14, all of that had happened while she was asleep. During the night. In the dark. But the 14 year version was as bright and sunny a day as it could get.

The other possible explanation was hallucination or dreaming.

Ok, alcohol can cause that, she agreed. But... it didn't feel like a dream or hallucination at all.

It felt too real.

All the feelings and emotions that came with the whole scenario felt too real. Felt too personal. She was able to touch everything, she was able to feel the frustration and despair that she was going through. Very vividly. And very, very strongly. She could still mildly feel the sting where she had hit her head while wreaking havoc in principal's office.

It could not have been just a dream. She was sure of that.

There was something else at play here. Something bigger than her. There was no denying that.

And in everything that was going on, she felt like she was merely being used as a pawn. Don't ask her how she knew that... she just did.

It was as if the world itself was telling her that something was amiss.

And then, there was that other tiny thing too, that was constantly nagging at the back of her mind.

She could suddenly sense people's emotions and feelings.

That how she could really tell what Dr. Martin was thinking about her situation, about believing her or not. The both of them. She had never been able to that earlier, ever. But nor, it was like their thoughts and emotions laid bare before her, unless someone was actively trying to deliberately hide it. And it hadn't been like that just with the doctor though, she had been able to feel everyone that she had come across since waking up in the morning.

It was like some floodgates were opened, after being closed for a very long time.

It was confusing. And overwhelming. Very much so.

She did not know what to do about it, yet.

So she let it be for now. First she needed to focus on the out of body experience thing. And what exactly to do about it.

Because by now she had realized that it was not going to be just a one-time thing.

It had started happening a week ago, right on her birthday, and was going on continuously, never stopping once. And now that she had fully entered that world, whatever it was, she doubted that she would stop doing so. She had even started to remember all the tiny details of those dreams that she had been missing beforehand. And she could not just leave that be, she needed to find the root of the problem and fix it before it got even bigger.

What if she never woke up from those dreams one day?

What if she got stuck in that world forever?

Those were some scary thoughts she did not want to come true.

'*Research...*' her mind supplied, or more like the word came to her unbidden as if the world itself whispered to her, as she thought about where to start. So if the world wanted her to research, she would research. For that, she was going to need to contact one person she had never thought she willingly, without any emergency, would. But maybe it was an emergency in itself... so she got to call her mother.

Something told her that's where she would fine her answers.

That everything was linked to her family somehow.

How? She did not know that just yet.

But she would soon find out.

CHAPTER 8

Amaria had called her mother and told her about the weird dreams that she was having and asked her if she had idea about why it was happening to her. She gathered that if it was due to her alcoholism her mother would know best. Or id it was something genetic, again her mother would know best.

And her mother, she had promptly disconnected the call after knowing the reason why she was calling her.

Weird but not really surprising.

So instead, Amaria had decide to pay her dear mother a visit, in person. If she wasn't willing to talk to her on phone.

Because her reaction to the information had told Amaria that her mother knew something that she did not.

And she was proven right.

Amaria and her mother had never seen eye to eye, they had never even had a chance to do so. The very first memories of her mother that Amaria had, all consisted of her being dismissive of her, even going as far as derogatory some times.

The very first feeling she remembered having about her mother, was fear. And hope. Hope that this time around it would be different. Hope that if she just behaved like a good girl, if she just studied better, her mother would notice. And she would be proud of her and start liking her.

In hindsight it all seemed really stupid but what did she know, she was a kid, she was allowed to be stupid. And hopeful.

But it wasn't too long when only the fear remained after and there was no hope left, whatsoever. Because no matter how hard she tried, or how good she behaved, she had never been able to get her mother's attention and care. So she stopped doing so. And she stopped caring.

Her mother was never present for any important day or event in her life, not even her birthdays. In fact, she never even remembered having a birthday celebration and that's because she never did. She probably wouldn't have even known when her birthday was if it wasn't for her birth certificate and her school documents. She always thought it was because her mother had hated her, she just did not know why that was the case. What had she done to warrant that hate?

It hadn't been much, much later when she had learned of the reason.

It was her father,

She had known her father was not in the picture earlier on. She had come to know that he had passed away the day she had first gotten admission in her school, where her mother had to tell the school that her father had passed away.

And even then, the reason of his demise, she wouldn't come to know till much later on.

On the day that she had finally broken down and aske her mother about her attitude, shouted and demanded to know the reason behind it, was the day everything had made sense to her. Well, not much but still, she had gotten to know the reason at least.

It was because her mother held her responsible for the death of her father.

Her father was on the way to the hospital, the day she was born, to come be with her mother as she was in labor. Unfortunately, he hadn't been able to make it.

He had been in a road accident and had died on the spot, right when she was born.

It had led her mother to avoid her because Amaria was the reminder of her loss.

It had brought Amaria immense grief after knowing the real reason, she might have gotten on the self-hate wagon too, holding herself the cause, if it wasn't for her friends. Kevin and Gabriella. They had been there for her then convincing her that it was that driver's fault who was drunk driving and had ended up killing her father. That she should not hold herself accountable for someone else's fault. Wise words those were, so she agreed.

It had then brought intense relief to Amaria, knowing that she was at least loved for a while, even if it was before she was actually born.

That was the row that had been the last straw for their relationship. They were beyond any recovery by then so Amaria had chosen to instead pack up and leave that house and that mother behind, never to look behind again.

She moved out and moved on with her life, not having any idea that she would be brought right back there once again.

And this time around, the row between them had been even more explosive.

This time around she had found things about her and her family history that she had never even imagined.

Amaria belonged to a long line of witches.

Ok, maybe calling them witches was an overkill but, that was the word that came to her mind on hearing the truth. In actuality, the females in Amaria's family, from her mother's side, all carried some sort of magic. A supernatural ability in them, be it putting on curses or charms, seeing the future or even reading people's minds or emotions.

Apparently Now Amaria had shown that she was one of those supernatural beings too. She was a dark empath, according to her mother and her verdict after listening to her explaining what she was feeling around other people.

All of it was very fascinating For Amaria. She had never thought that magic could be real, and maybe it wasn't, in the traditional sense of the meaning, but it was magical enough for her, that people like her existed in the world.

The day also revealed another reason her mother was dismissive of her.

The day she was born, her mother had lost her own magical ability. Her mother who had been always excellent at putting up some small charms here and there, never could after that day.

'Just another reason for her to hate me...' thought Amaria despondently as she practically dropped on her bed after such a hectic day.

She had no energy left in her to fight and stay awake for any more. She knew she would have to sleep sooner rather than later. As much as the day had been enlightening, it was also somewhat of a bust somehow. She had gotten to know a lot about her family but she still did not know anything about her waking dreams. But at least she now had an idea what and where to look for.

Her family. She did not have to go far. She just needed to do some more background research on her family and find where the signs led her to.

But first, she had to sleep.

She knew another world would be waiting for her on the other side of the consciousness. But this time around, she was ready to embrace it.

Called The Girl With The Broken Spirit

CHAPTER 9

Undertaking

Amaria was not prepared for it.

No matter how much she told herself that, the truth of the reality was that she was not ready to face the dream world.

She had just been more expectant of it is all.

Facing her mother after the last night's row with her, was not going to be easy. And knowing what she knew now, it made her see her mother in a whole new light and she was not ready to come to terms with that knowledge just yet.

After spending her whole life with resentment and indifference, caring or more like feeling empathy for her suddenly seemed next to impossible.

So she took the coward's way out and just disappeared from the house as soon as she possibly could after waking up as 14.

Unfortunately, her options were quite limited, and by that it meant that her only option was school. So off to the school she went.

Surprisingly, or rather unsurprisingly, it was the very next day in her dream world too. And that meant that everyone at school remembered her breakdown the previous day. And by the looks that were thrown at her, as soon as she entered the building, it was clear as the day that she was deemed hysterical, someone who had surely lost her marbles.

It was not, admittedly, a very good feeling, to be seen as an interesting specimen. Or more like attention seeking, if the word of the mouth was to be believed.

Soon enough though, she caught up with her friends, Gabriella; or Gabby as she liked to call her, and Kevin; also known as Kev sometimes.

"Ams…!" She heard the shout of her name from a mile away, and probably so did everyone else. It was Kevin, as usual, he was the only one who called her that. Almost everyone else, who was close enough at least, preferred to just shorten her name from Amaria to Maria.

She turned around and got an armful of the said boy, he was hugging the daylights out of her. Gaby had to intervene and pull him away from her, only to take his place instead. Her hug was far more gentle and tentative though.

And that's how it had always been, hadn't it?

Amaria was the emotionally constipated one, most of the times, Gabriella was the mature and understanding one. And Kevin? Well, he was the wild card of their team. He was prone to doing something totally unexpected at random. Or maybe not really unexpected because they were expecting him to do something unexpected anyway? Oh well, semantics.

Being there with them once again, feeling their care and warmth, made her tear up again, and causing them to get alarmed once again in turn. She had to hurriedly assure them that she was fine. That those were just happy tears.

They were sceptic but let it go, instead asking her what had gone wrong the previous day. According to them they had even gone to her house after school but she wasn't there. And when Kevin had come to check up on her later in the night, her mother had told him she was asleep. So they were pretty curious to know what had happened to her to cause the sudden breakdown.

Seeing their concern and care for her made her stop and think about her circumstances some more. She did not know how long this whole situation was going to go on and she came to the sudden realization that she could not go through this alone. Dr. Martin had been of no help to her this time around but maybe, her friends could be the ones she could rely on.

That was a thought. She could tell them!

Maybe not the whole travelling between the worlds thing, explaining someone that they just might be the figment of her imagination was bound to be hard. And very uncomfortable. But, she could at least tell them about her family legacy and the whole magical being thing. They might be of help in researching more about her family history, if nothing else.

Her mind made up, she took a deep breath and came to a resolve. She was going to tell them.

She grabbed both of them by their hands and, dragging them behind her, headed straight to find a secluded and empty spot. For them it had always been under the bleachers of the stadium or on the rooftop of the school after Kevin had learned to pick a lock.

For now though, bleachers it was.

She took them all the way there, dismissing their surprise at the sudden action and their protests. Classes could wait, in her opinion. This was definitely far more important.

And when she told them about it all, her birth and her strange power and the line of supernatural women in her family, they seemed to agree on that too. It was definitely more important. And far more interesting in Kevin's opinion.

She was just thankful that they were leaning more towards believing her, instead of mocking her or calling her delusional, like many others would if it got out.

There might also be the opposite case that might come true. That people would believe her and then start fearing her. Or even hating her. So there was fine line to walk on. And her friends? They had just proven to be the best case there could be. They believed her and did not seem to fear her, or see her any differently. For them it was just a cool new thing, she was the same girl they had always been friends with.

But now, with this new information, there came a new task too. Searching about Amaria's family history. Without telling her mother, of course. This version of her had never told Amaria anything about their lineage, so talking to her would only make her suspicious and angry.

So sitting there, thinking and talking about it, they came up with the next course of action. They had an almost full day ahead of them for getting all the information they needed. They were going to scourge the libraries, both school and local for any relative information, newspapers, family registries and even her house.

More specifically her mother's stuff at her house.

This time around, she was going to find everything out by herself first, get to the bottom of it all, and then approach Dr. Martin. He will have no choice but to believe her then and, hopefully, help her too.

With that thought in her mind they set off to the work.

They had a lot of digging to do. Hopefully not the actual, physical kind though.

CHAPTER 10

The Reveal

Amaria and her friends took to the research as if their life depended it, which it probably did for Amaria in a way, and they searched high and low for any morsel of information that they could get their hands on.

Soon enough they had discovered everything there was to know about her family. From her mother's documents and some old letters and stuff, Amaria had come to know that there had been a row in the family some generations back over a piece of land and the family had scattered after that. It was her great, great grandmother's property but her kids wanted to get their hands on it. They wanted to sell the land and get their portion of the money. It had been a huge family scandal at that time but ultimately the kids had forced their mother to give them the land.

The notes said that they had kicked her out for the land. But the most agreed upon consensus was that the woman had just left after signing off the property and was never seen again. Her kids sold the land and moved on with their own separate lives. It seemed that they had never reconnected again and it had become a sort of a tradition in the family that after growing up the kids and the parents would get separated, never to reconnect again.

The same had been the case with Amaria's mother and her own mother, Amaria's grandmother. They had drifted apart after her mother had gotten married and weren't even in touch anymore.

That was what made Amaria the most curious. Why did the parents and the children always drift off? That had been her case too. After moving away from home, in her adult life, she had almost fully lost touch with her mother and she was pretty sure it would have been a full disconnection between them if the sudden strange events hadn't started happening.

But still, that was a thought to ponder on.

But later on.

First, she wanted to try and find her grandmother.

She had always thought that most of her extended family was dead, just like her father, and that was the reason why she had never met them. She had only ever met an uncle of hers, her mother's brother, but not much either. She had always wanted a big family and lots of relatives and cousins to celebrate life with but sadly it was never the case for her.

Suddenly finding out that she might have some family spread out in the world seemed like a second chance for her. Especially her grandmother. She really wanted to find her, as a grandmother as well as a possible guide in her spiritual journey. She knew she could never ask her mother to help her through her new abilities but maybe she could ask her grandmother for that help instead. She was bound to be even more knowledgeable than her mother. She was a long practicing magical being and apparently she was a master at healing and potions. She thought that as the most fascinating tidbit of information that she had found while looking through her mother's things.

Her mind made up, she convinced her friends to look for her grandmother next. Unfortunately, they had no ground to start from as there was no information anywhere about her recent hereabouts. Her last letter to her mother was over a decade old so they weren't even sure if she lived at the same place.

Deciding to give it a chance anyway, they set off for the address written on the letter. It was about half an hour of bus ride away from her place so they thought that night be the best shot they had so why not give it a go. Hoping for the best to come out of that short trip.

Unfortunately, their hopes were squashed when they reached the listed house.

Her grandmother did not live there.

She had moved from there about 7 years ago and the residents of that house had changed twice after she had left so she couldn't even get any kind of new address for her.

It was a complete dead end.

Dejected at the bust and the lost time, they returned back home.

It was on the way home from the bus stop when a strange idea started taking home in her mind. She wasn't sure about it but she had to give it a go.

She turned towards Kevin and Gaby, ready to tell them her new plan, when she noticed how tired and worried both of them looked. It was already nearing the evening and she realized that they must have been worrying about their parents and getting home. They had been away for the whole day so it was understandable. She decided to spare them any more hassle and told them to go back home, calling it a day.

They readily agreed, assuring her that everything would be fine and not to worry and she nodded with a grateful smile, thankful for all their help.

After leaving them at their respective houses, she was left alone to walk towards her own house.

But something kept nagging at him, urging her to act upon her thoughts. It wasn't like her mother would miss her, or even notice that she was gone from the house, she reasoned to herself.

She stopped in her tracks, took in a deep breath and turned on her feet.

Back towards where she was coming from.

She almost ran to the main road. Stopping an incoming taxy, she immediately shouted out the destination in her mind.

It was the place her family dispute had been over, generations ago.

She was going to visit that piece of land and see what had happened to it. Something in her had urged her to go check that out. She had an inkling that it was going to be the place where she would find all her answers. She hoped that her sixth sense wasn't just playing games with her.

She hoped that it wouldn't prove to be just a wild goose chase.

CHAPTER 11

Luna

That night Amaria came back home disappointed.

She had reached the place that had been the cause of conflict in her family, only to find it desolate. It was a barren piece of land with nothing in sight. There was no building on it, no trees or plants, not even a boundary wall or anything like that. She found it extremely odd, considering that a huge commotion was once caused because of it and now it was as if it laid ownerless.

She did feel a pull towards it once she turned around to get back home. And for the life of her she could not understand what exactly was pulling her towards the place. She gave it another once over, and still finding nothing, she turned away and started on her way home.

Now she was lying in her bed, trying to focus on falling asleep, instead of on the events of the day.

71

She now needed to wake up in her own world and do some digging there. She kept thinking what to do next and how to get in contact with her grandmother when the sleep came and took her in.

She woke up with a blaring alarm and a raging headache, again. And she hadn't even been drinking last night! It was honestly starting to concern her a little bit. Was it a side effect of her magic or something?

But whatever it might be, she didn't have time to ponder on that right now. She had some rather important issues to attend to. Namely, finding her grandmother.

She decided to go with her gut feeling for the day. There was definitely a time difference or something between her two worlds, so there was a chance for her inkling to be true in this world. She needed to get to her ancestral place and see if she could find anything there.

So, she called in sick, threw on the first reasonable piece of clothing she came across, grabbed a toast and some juice and she was out the house. On her way to the same place she had been last night.

Only this time around, she had more anticipation and nerves buzzing in her body. She didn't want it to be a dead end again.

Whoever deity that she had been praying to, must have been listening.

She was standing there in front of the land, checking and double checking that it was the right place and yes, it was definitely the right place. Only it looked mighty different than the last time she had seen it.

There was a small shop there with a very rustic charm to it. It was plain and simple from the outside, no fancy bits or baubles. There weren't even any windows or anything. There was a small wooden board on the side of the door that displayed its name on it in Old English.

"The Mystique Dame"

Amaria felt in her heart then and there, she had finally come where she was supposed to be.

She went to knock on the door but found it already open. Taking a deep breath to settle her nerves, she pushed the door open and stepped inside.

It was magical.

There wasn't just one type of thing to sell in there, the shop had a lot of peculiar stuff spread throughout it. There were so many old books lining one wall, and so many odd trinkets another. There were so many different flowers and leaves in beautiful, robust colors, definitely more than she had ever seen in her life. There were herbs and roots and simmering potion cauldrons. And so much more.

She was just looking around the place, struck by the very mystical feeling it gave off, when suddenly a woman appeared through the back door holding iridescent purplish flowers in her hands. Almost bursting in, she came to a halt when she saw Amaria. It was an old woman with completely white hair and wearing an even whiter flowing tunic.

"I have been expecting you." She said, calmly walking towards Amaria.

"I'm sorry what...?" Amaria asked, sure that she hadn't booked any sort of appointment beforehand for the woman to expect her.

The woman went to a table that was already covered in flowers and placed the new ones on there too. Then she turned fully turned towards Amaria, giving her a once over and taking her in.

"The spirits told me that you were coming. Although they did tell me this last night and I kept waiting the whole night. You did not come."

"...What?" Amaria asked, now thoroughly spooked.

"Hmm..." the woman kept looking at her as if looking for something. And then suddenly something dawned in her.

"But you did come last night. Didn't you...? Just that here was not this here."

"How... How do you know all this?"

"Oh I should probably introduce myself first..." she started coming closer to Amaria until she was standing almost nose to nose with her.

"I'm Luna. Your grandmother."

Amaria stood there, not knowing if she should be shocked or relieved at that when the woman took the choice out of her hands and took her by the arm, pulling her towards the back door.

"Come on, I have to show you something."

And after everything Amaria had been through, who was she to question. So she went along.

And boy was she glad that she did.

As soon as she stepped out of the door, she felt like she had been transported to heaven. Or at least a fairytale. Because the place was not much less than the Garden of Eden itself.

It was the most beautiful garden she had laid her eyes on. The trees, the leaves, the flowers, everything seemed to be emanating a soft glow. They were pink and purple, and so many other colors. And they were pretty and perfect.

There were hundreds of butterflies, just as ethereal and just as glowing, going from flower to flower. Some even came to her, fluttering close to her face and that's when she realized that they were actually small pixies. She reached to touch one of them but it quickly fluttered away, along with all the others, hiding in between the trees and away from her sight.

The woman, her grandmother, swatted her hand and that quickly brought her out of her daze.

"No touching. They are shy" she said, as if that explained everything. As if that was the only question she had in mind.

"Welcome to the garden of serenity" she said, gesturing around her.

And oh… maybe that did explain everything.

She did feel very serene after all.

Called The Girl With The Broken Spirit

CHAPTER 12

The Darkest Hour

The Garden of serenity really proved to be the answer to it all.

Just not in the sense that she was hoping for.

Because according to her grandmother, she was cursed. And so was the whole bloodline. Luna had found it out when she purchased the land that had once belonged to their ancestor. She did not know it initially but just as Amaria had, she had also felt the place calling to her and she had answered that call. The land had been barren then too, when she had first found it. The only thing there was a magical tree planted there decades ago. It appeared normal but she knew it was magical with just one look at it.

When she researched it and dug up around it, she found out that it was a source of a curse. A curse that was put upon the whole family, none other than the original owner of the place herself.

And it couldn't be removed.

Their ancestor, Thelma, when forced to give away her land, decided to take revenge on everyone. So she put the whole bloodline under a curse. A very peculiar and a very scary one, to say the least.

It entailed that every one of them would experience a trauma, like Thelma once did, by the age of 25. And that trauma would later manifest itself in a lasting agony when they would turn 25. It could be in any way possible. Amaria's had made her create another dimension to practically relive it because hers' was particularly strong.

Amaria was actually blown away by the creativity of the curse, and very pissed too.

She wasn't the one who took away the land, why was she the one suffering?

She laid in her bed and pondered this question, as she started drifting off to sleep.

She woke up, and you guessed it, she was 16. She followed the old mundane routine, had some words with her mother, had breakfast and got ready and got to school.

For once she went to class in school, instead of running around, chasing one answer or the other. Now she had all the answers in front of her, she just needed to figure out what to do with them. She also focused on spending some quality time with Gabriella and Kevin, she didn't know what was to come so she decided to take advantage of what the time had given her.

It was proving out be rather marvelous.

So much so that she had almost forgotten where she was and what the stakes of her being there were.

She was going back to her class after going to the loo, humming a low tone under her breath, when the next unexpected hit her. A hand grabbed her arm roughly as she was passing through an alcove and almost dragged her in and through the hidden door of the unused classroom.

A room where she had been in before, many a times.

The room of her worst nightmares.

The room where her biggest trauma belonged.

And sure enough, when she looked at the person the hand was attached to, it was the face that had caused her, that biggest trauma of hers.

He was one of the reasons she was trapped in the curse.

He was getting all handsy with her, touching and rubbing and squishing whatever and wherever he could reach.

And she stood there, trapped in her past. She remembered that. She remembered how it had started when she was just a kid, the man was her neighbor. She had remembered how it had progressed further and further, the man was now her teacher in school. She also remembered telling her mother about it but to no affect. Her mother had just looked at her in disdain and replied that she probably deserved it.

That she was probably asking for it.

She was not.

She wasn't asking for it now either.

But it was still happening, only she wasn't defenseless child now.

Now she was just feeling a rage so intense she saw black.

And when she next came to, there were no hands caressing her.

There was, however, blood dripping from her. Blood that now also painted that room.

Blood that came out of that man.

That man who was now lying at her feet. Dead. And in pieces.

And there were shadows wrapping around her, growling and hissing. Going out of control and then retreating back in her.

And she had done it. Her magic did.

As soon as she realized that, she felt like she couldn't breathe anymore. She fell to her knees in shock and hurled the contents of her breakfast in disgust and despair.

And then she rushed out of the room and into the school corridors, drenched in blood, with tears streaming down her face. The look on her face could only be described as deranged. She didn't think she could bear it anymore, not after what she had just done. Not if she could do even worse, to someone dearer. She just wanted to get out of that damned cursed world. And for that, she just had one destination in mind, the counselors' office.

Dr. Martin's office.

She banged open the door as soon as she reached the office. Doctor Martin quickly raised his head from where he was reading something on his table, surprised at the sudden interruption.

"Wha__" he started but couldn't finish his sentence, Amira cut him off breathlessly.

"You have to send me home, Dr. Martin! I need to get out of this place right now!" She cried out, hiccupping and panicking.

"Uh... do you want me to call your home and have someone come and get you? Why do... is that blood? What happened!? Are you hurt somewhere Miss. Garcia!?" he quickly stood up, rushing to her and examining her, looking for any wounds.

"No, no, no... just... you have to put me to sleep Dr. Martin! I need to go back to my world...!" She rushed out her words, begging him to understand her.

"Miss Garcia... I'm afraid I don't follow what you are trying to say. Is this about the other day? Are you still having those dream issues you mentioned?" he asked, puzzled.

Amaria took in a little breath, trying to calm herself down.

"Look… I know you don't believe me Dr. Martin, but please… I beg of you… please put me to sleep. I know you can easily do it, you have already done it to me plenty of times before. So please… just this once, trust me on this please, Dr. Martin."

Dr. Martin observed her face for a while, silently, searching for something and he must have found that something as he let out a resigned sigh and motioned her to sit on the couch.

He was going to make her sleep.

And he did.

And as he was doing so, she hoped and wished and prayed that she would never wake up in this world again.

She promised herself that she would not come back here as she fell asleep.

And then she woke up.

Just as panicked

Just as devastated.

She needed to talk to someone. She didn't know her grandma enough just yet to tell her and her mother was out of the question. The only other name that came to her mind was Dr. Martin.

She knew he had started believing in her a little bit, if his frequent texts and calls regarding her dreams and everything were to go by. And she knew she could trust him. He already knew all of her secrets. He knew about all her deep rooted traumas and fears so he would at least understand why… it had happened.

So she hit him up to meet her in his office, and she was out the door. Going to the same office herself.

This time, she would come back home without any curse, or never come back at all, she decided.

CHAPTER 13

The Conclusion

Amaria was sitting in Dr. Martin's office and telling him everything from A to Z once again. With much conviction and all the facts behind it all. And she knew he believed her this time around.

And with the condition that she was in, there weren't many chances of him not believing her.

She was crying inconsolably, wishing for everything to get right again. She was going out of control, and so were her powers, the flickering lights and the very still but still howling air around her was a dead giveaway. She had started to get engulfed in the swirling shadows around her, so much so that it seemed like she was the one emitting them, instead of getting immersed in them.

It was suffocating.

And she did not know how much longer she could take it, without getting choked in the oppressing darkness surrounding her, or worse, taking someone else with her too.

Dr. Martin seemed to have come to the same understanding. He abruptly stood up and taking her hand, he pulled her to her feet too.

"Come on, we are going to get you better Amaria and I know just the place for it."

With that they were out the office and out the building, Amaria diligently following him. In that one moment she realized how desperate she was becoming. She thought she could have followed him to the end of the earth if it meant she would be saved. If the course could get lifted from her.

It was as much concerning as it was devastating.

Dr. Martin took her to the car and set off to a destination still unknown to her, rash and determined.

They came to a stop in front of the church.

Amaria stared at it, suddenly realizing what the plan Dr. Martin had in mind was. Suddenly realizing what was to happen. She swirled her head to look at him. He was still resolutely looking ahead, not sparing her a look.

"I think this might be our only option Amaria. And you know that too." He said, as if in answer to the silent questions in her eyes.

He got out of the car and so did Amaria. They walked together to the front gates of the church, ready to open the doors when suddenly they were interrupted by the screeching halt of another car. They turned around to see who it might be, this late in the night.

It was her grandmother, getting out of the car.

And lo and behold, her mother was right there too.

Her shock must have shown on her face because her grandmother was quick to give her the reason of their visit.

"The spirits were telling me I needed to be here. They just about forced me to come her, and bring her along. And now I understand why. You are here to get rid of the curse." She told them all matter of fact, as if it made perfect sense.

Without giving them any time to continue the conversation, her grandmother briskly walked ahead of them and into the church.

They followed her in too, wondering what the night was going to bring them next.

A lot.

The night brought them a lot.

Most of it went as a blur for Amaria. A string of random, unknown words thrown together to make an answer she still couldn't bring herself to believe possible.

The priest was of the opinion that it was possible to get rid of her curse after all. They just had to do an exorcism to get rid of the spirits tied with the curse. Because yes, there were spirits that secured the curse. That made sure the curse would befall the whole family line.

Getting rid of them would mean there would be no tethers of the curse left on their blood, making the curse disappear.

Amaria readily agreed, and so did her mother.

Her poor mother who was under the same curse as her, only it had appeared differently in her. She had lost the person she loved the most in the world, her husband, that was her trauma, and she had lost her magic, that was the result of her trauma.

They had reacted differently and similarly to their traumas. Both of them had become self-depreciating alcoholics as a result, disregarding everyone and everything. The difference had been that Amaria was willing to fight to get herself back, but now her mother was too.

As she was the latest victim, the spirits were latched onto her so, Amaria stepped up and the exorcism officially became.

The rite was gentle at first, just involving spoken prayers and some readings from the scripture and sometimes even the gentle touches to her head and heart. Soon though, it turned painful too, as if something inside of her was burning. She started screaming and thrashing at that, as her body itself began to fight the spirits and vice versa. There were people holding on to her tightly, so as not to make her hurt someone or herself physically. It was pure torture.

It was hell on earth.

It felt like hours, but it must have been few minute probably, but soon everything stopped altogether. There was no screaming, no hissing and no thrashing around. It went dead silent.

And then Amaria felt it.

She was free! Oh God, she was finally free of the curse!

She would never have to back to that retched place ever again.

She was so, so happy and relieved, feeling lighter than she had ever felt in life. As if the curse was a physical thing holding her down, and now all of a sudden she could jump and dance and scream of joy. So she did just that.

She jumped in pure elation and jumped right into Dr. Martin's arms who was the nearest. She hugged the daylights out of him. Thanking him repeatedly, tears of happiness freely flowing down her cheeks.

Her mother and grandmother seemed to be feeling the same, standing closer to each other, holding each other's hands with bittersweet smiles and misty eyes.

They were all so busy feeling the euphoria of the moment that none of them noticed the shadows that had just left Amaria creeping back again.

Latching back onto the target.

Only this time, the unsuspecting target was no witch.

It was Dr. Martin.

Made in the USA
Monee, IL
07 July 2026

56551420R00056